TO
ELSIE,
LOVE FROM

Hi, I'm
ELSIE!
What's your
name?

On a normal street like yours and mine,
It was a bright and sunny day.
Elsie opened the door, and suddenly saw,
A gang of animals waiting to play.

The tiger loves taking centre stage,
He's quite the confident one.
But equally, and I'm sure you'll agree,
His shy friends are also fun.

Let'sss play, ELSIE!

Hide-and-seek's a favourite game,
It's Elsie versus the giraffes.
Her careful disguise won't fool their eyes,
And it ends with smiles and laughs.

Here we come, ELSIE!

Some friends like to relax and snuggle,
Others creep about and are tickly.
The otters hug, the gorillas are snug,
And the porcupines are cute and prickly.

Wanna hug, ELSIE?

The sloths love hanging out and snoozing,
While the monkeys swing about.
Elsie happily grins at the jumps and spins,
And the wild and cheeky shouts.

ZZZZZZ

It's time to settle down for lunch,
Elsie's burger takes some beating.
Her friends have FRUITS,

GRASS, GRUBS and ROOTS,

There's an icky stench wafting
through the air,
And Elsie is turning greener!
It might just be, the hippo, you see,

Or perhaps the RING-TAILED LEMUR?!

Elsie spots the rhinos squabbling,
They're bickering and butting their heads.
She must put a stop, to their childish strop,
"I'll try a spot of juggling," she said.

Elsie's hair is a little bit messy,
"But my friends look much funnier!"
she thinks.

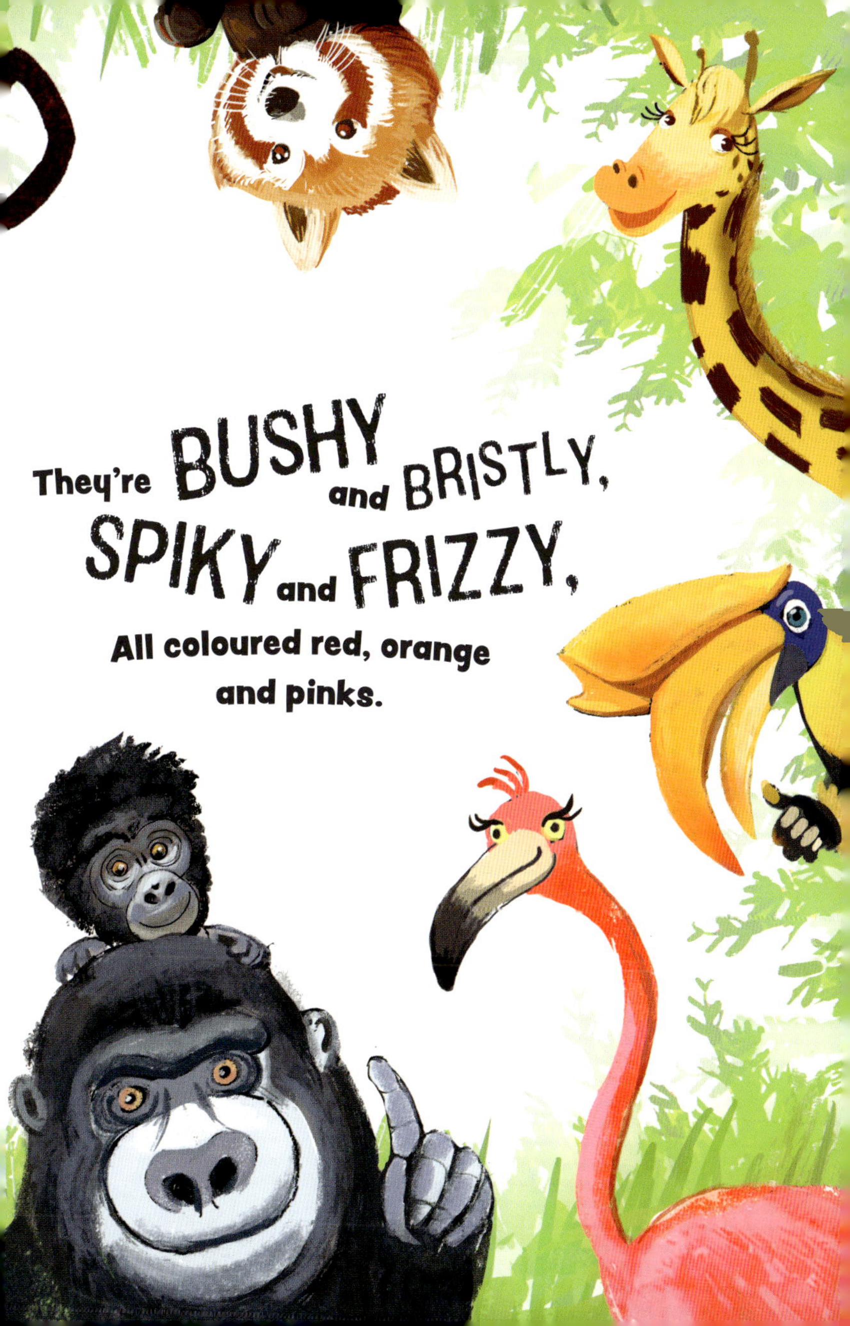

They're BUSHY and BRISTLY,
SPIKY and FRIZZY,

All coloured red, orange
and pinks.

Hooray! They've found a trampoline,
It's sure to raise a grin.

The giraffe takes flight,
And the hippo's a sight,
As they LEAP and

BOUNCE and SPRING.

Night night, ELSIE

Elsie is ready to head back home,
As night eclipses the day.
But there's still time,
For a little more rhyme,
As her friends have
SOMETHING TO
SAY....

She's fun!
She's clever!
She's friendly!
She's kind!
She really loves to play!

Elsie can't deny,
As she waves goodbye,

Elsie, now draw your different friends and tell us why they're so special.

Written by Joe Barnes
Illustrated by Cinzia Battistel
Designed by Alice Xavier

First published by HOMETOWN WORLD in 2019
Hometown World Ltd
1 Queen Street
Bath
BA1 1HE

Visit
www.hometownworld.co.uk

Follow us @hometownworldbooks

ISBN 978-1-78979-088-7

Printed in Italy
HTW_PO201910

Hometown World